Sketch for a Theory of the Emotions

'A driving force in all Sartre's writings is his serious desire to change the life of his reader.'

Iris Murdoch

'. . . a model of lucid exposition, very well translated. The central thesis stands out with tempting clarity . . . *Sketch for a Theory of the Emotions* is certainly the best introduction available to the world of *Being and Nothingness*, and is also a useful guide to M. Sartre's more difficult views on the imagination.'

The Times Literary Supplement

Routledge Classics contains the very best of Routledge publishing over the past century or so, books that have, by popular consent, become established as classics in their field. Drawing on a fantastic heritage of innovative writing published by Routledge and its associated imprints, this series makes available in attractive, affordable form some of the most important works of modern times.

For a complete list of titles visit
www.routledgeclassics.com

Jean-Paul
Sartre

Sketch for a Theory of the Emotions

Translated by Philip Mairet

With a preface by Mary Warnock

 London and New York

The original edition of this work was published in France
with the title: *Esquisse d'une théorie des emotions* by Les Editions
Scientifiques HERMANN, 1939. Copyright by Hermann, Paris.

English edition first published 1962
by Methuen & Co. Ltd
First published by Routledge 1994

First published in Routledge Classics 2002
by Routledge
2 Park Square, Milton Park, Abingdon, OX14 4RN
711 Third Avenue, New York, NY 10017 (8th Floor)

Routledge is an imprint of the Taylor & Francis Group, an informa business

English translation © 1962 Methuen & Co. Ltd
Preface © 1962 Methuen & Co. Ltd

Typeset in Joanna by RefineCatch Limited, Bungay, Suffolk

British Library Cataloguing in Publication Data
A catalogue record for this book is available from the British Library

ISBN10: 0–415–26751–X (hbk)
ISBN10: 0–415–26752–8 (pbk)

ISBN13: 978–0–415–26751–9 (hbk)
ISBN13: 978–0–415–26752–6 (pbk)

CONTENTS

PREFACE

by Mary Warnock

The Esquisse d'une théorie des émotions was published in Paris in 1939, when Sartre was thirty-four. The essay is the best source for Sartre's theoretical views on the nature of psychology, and it contains doctrines which were later incorporated, though without such full discussion of their origin, in his major work L'Etre et le Néant. It is therefore well worth reading as a preparation for the longer book; but it is also capable of standing on its own as a document in the history both of phenomenology and of existentialism. English readers may be uncertain whether to classify it as an essay in psychology or in philosophy; but they could remind themselves that there is the same ambiguity in the works of Hume, as well as in those of the phenomenologists, and of Husserl in particular, from whom Sartre derived so much.

The essay starts with a criticism of the accounts of the emotions offered by psychological theory from William James onwards. James held a theory known as Peripheric . . . that emotion is the consciousness of physiological disturbance. Thus, on this theory, to speak of an emotion causing physical symptoms in the person who feels it is to put the cart before the horse. Sadness does not cause tears; on the contrary, James prefers paradoxically to say that the tears, the physiological disturbance, cause the sadness, which is the consciousness of this disturbance. This view was criticized, by Sartre and others, for its inadequacy when faced with the problem of distinguishing one emotion from another, and for its failure to account for the plain facts. There is too great an element of thought, and thought of an object, in sadness or in anger for either to be satisfactorily analysed as the presentation to consciousness of a physical change.

Janet's theory is treated more sympathetically by Sartre. Janet treats emotion as a twofold kind of behaviour, consisting both of mental and of physical phenomena. He attempts to account for both elements by defining emotion as the behaviour of defeat. In the example discussed in this essay, a girl breaks down in tears because the alternative, discussing her case with her doctor, is too difficult for her. Weeping is an easier substitute. Sartre argues against this view that it illegitimately introduces the concept of finality, or purposiveness. His own definition of emotion itself contains this concept, but his point against Janet is that his account has no business to introduce purposiveness since it does not also introduce consciousness or awareness of any kind into the definition. Janet fails, according to Sartre, to show that the mental element in emotion, as he describes it, is such as to be capable of supporting the idea of a purpose. The mental element here, as in the peripheric theory, is not sufficiently cognitive. If behaviour is to be purposive, there must be an end actually *in view*. Incidentally, the criticism of Janet is highly characteristic of Sartre's style . . . the anecdotal style. Moreover, his preferred account of the girl and her doctor is that she weeps *in order not* to have to talk to him, although she half believes that she wants to do so; and thus she is presented as self deceiving, behaving in bad faith, in a manner which plays an important part in Sartre's theory of human nature in *L'Etre et le Néant*, and which is richly illustrated there. The reason for preferring this account, Sartre says, is that it quite explicitly employs the concept of purpose, by treating emotions as an 'organized pattern of means directed to an end'.

Dembo's theory, in Sartre's view, comes even nearer to a true account of the emotions. According to this theory anger, for instance, is an alternative way out of a difficulty when all other ways are blocked. It is the resort of frustration. And so with the other emotions. But it is an essentially inferior way out . . . a means adopted towards an end, but by an inferior part of ourselves. We become less critical of ourselves in moments of frustration and therefore we are prepared to make use of means which normally we should reject. This account, Sartre says, is perfect, but still insufficient. For, he argues, there could be no change from one (superior) form of behaviour to another (inferior) without consciousness. One form of behaviour cannot take over from another unless 'it presents itself clearly as the substitute for the previous form'. It is necessary, therefore, to have recourse explicitly to the consciousness, as soon as it is realized that an account of emotion must describe a certain relation between the subject and the world outside him. Thus James and Janet and Dembo are represented by Sartre as moving through decreasingly inadequate theories to the conclusion that emotion can be described only in cognitive terms, or in terms of consciousness.

What exactly does Sartre understand by the word 'consciousness'? Until this is clear there is no hope of understanding the positive part of his doctrine. After the critical account of the theories we have so far noticed, Sartre goes on to an attempted refutation of the 'psychoanalytic' theory or the theory of the unconscious, and in this passage his own concept of the consciousness becomes clearer, though it must be said that it is never entirely clear. (Incidentally, it should be noticed that Sartre is concerned above all to substitute his own theory for Freud's, and that some of the most powerful passages in *L'Etre et le Néant* are directed towards the same end.)

To accept the doctrine of the unconscious, he says, is to reject Cartesianism, and he implies that this is something that no sane man would do. Cartesianism is his name for a certain view of consciousness, the view, briefly, that consciousness must necessarily always be aware of itself. It will be seen at once that if consciousness is defined as that which is aware of being conscious, or aware of itself, then the notion of the unconscious is contradictory. Sartre claims to derive this definition, with its anti-Freudian consequence, from Descartes' well-known argument known as the *cogito* argument. Descartes, having decided to trust neither his senses nor what he had learned from other people, found that he could not doubt his own existence, whatever else he doubted, since he proved his own existence as a cognitive being every time he doubted, or indulged in any other mental activity. The basis of his system of philosophy, therefore, was the proposition that he existed as a thinking being. Now this argument has been interpreted in a number of different ways, some of them very far-fetched, and the numerous variations in the expression of it to be found in Descartes' own writing make it a peculiarly fruitful starting point for other philosophers. Indeed it has become a kind of act of piety with the French at least to claim to derive their own position from his. But it would be most unplausible to hold that Sartre's view of consciousness or anything like it is really to be found in the writings of Descartes. Consciousness in the Sartrian sense is a product of phenomenology and though the phenomenologists thought of themselves as Cartesians, it is in fact misleading to use this title for them.

For Descartes argued that he could be certain of nothing except that he was a thinking being; as such he had ideas. The question which it was most urgent for him to solve was therefore the question of what clue these ideas gave him to the external world. Did they truly represent things as they were? His most important contribution to philosophy, for good or ill, was the raising of this question in this form. His own answer to it was on the whole unadventurous, and less important . . . namely, that generally we can trust our ideas to be true representations of things, if we take care to concentrate upon clear and distinct ideas. Further, that one of the ideas we *can* trust is the idea of a beneficent, non-deceiving God, who would not let us be always deceived in our other ideas. This is not the place to elaborate Descartes' arguments: the essential point for him was the separation between thought and its object, in such a way that the crucial question must be the truth or falsity of the thought, the reality or unreality of the object.

He did also argue however, though this was not central to his thesis, that since all my knowledge comes through my mind, I must necessarily know my mind better than anything else, especially better than my body. Now this minor and highly dubious argument could be said to give rise to the view of consciousness which we are trying to elucidate, for it might suggest that at the same time as being aware of an object, I must also be aware of my mind perceiving that object. This was the point upon which Husserl and the other phenomenologists fastened in their reading of Descartes. The essential feature of mental activity, for them, was that it had an object (was intensional) and that it could be reflexive. The true study of epistemology, and of the theory of perception, as well as of psychology proper was, in their view, to be carried out by disregarding the object of the mental act of e.g. perception, and concentrating instead on the act itself. In the case of any mental activity whatever it was necessary that there should be an object of it; but the proper course of philosophers was to perform an act of abstraction (*epoché*) so as to rule the object out and concentrate only upon the activity itself. This is the process known as 'putting the world in brackets'. There were some phenomenologists, such as Brentano, who regarded the philosophical task thereafter as a matter of pure description. Husserl, on the other hand, held that by performing this act of abstraction and concentrating each upon his own consciousness, philosophers could reach a universal general and absolute truth. Into this idealism we need not, fortunately, pursue him in the present context.[1]

In the argument against the unconscious in the present

---

[1] An extremely clear and useful account of the more important doctrines of phenomenology, together with some essays by Brentano and Husserl, is to be found in R. Chisholm's *Realism and the Background of Phenomenology* (London, 1961). For the relation between these doctrines and Existentialism, see the introduction to *Phenomenologie de la perception* by Maurice Merleau-Ponty (Paris, 1945).

essay, Sartre seems to go further than his so-called Cartesianism would warrant, in suggesting that consciousness must *always* be aware of itself, not just that it can be sometimes. But he admits that this knowledge need not always be perfectly explicit. And furthermore, the awareness of being aware which I have when I perceive something is what Sartre sometimes calls the *prereflective cogito*. It does not take the self as an object. It is not reflective, but simply goes along with, or accompanies my perceptions. This notion is far more Kantian than Cartesian. It recalls the I-thinking, the vehicle of all concepts, the transcendental I. But the main point against Freud is here made in terms of what will count as a possible *explanation* of conscious phenomena.

The explanation of any thought or dream or feeling must be sought, he says, not outside consciousness but within it, for instance in some purpose framed by the same mind, or in some object deliberately *meant* by it. Consciousness is not regarded as a *thing* like a stone or a pond. It is always directed on to something, it always means something. So an emotion which is part of my mental life means something by being directed towards some object of its own. It can be explained only in terms of this object, just as my words can be explained in terms of what they signify, what I mean by them, and not by any causal or inductively established relation which may be found experimentally to hold between my utterance and the external world. (Words are not like stones or ponds either.) The Freudians are held to be wrong because they overlook the intensionality of mental events, and think that there can be an inductively determined causal relation between my dream, let us say, and some external object . . . a relation of which I, the patient, am not aware since the connection is made by me subconsciously. So the argument against bare causal explanations of mental phenomena and against the unconscious come to the same.

Having disposed of Freud, Sartre comes to the positive doctrine: Emotions, like all other mental acts, are directed towards an object. It is impossible to discuss an emotion without mentioning both the object and the subject who regards this object in a certain light, e.g. as hateful. 'The emotion is a specific manner of apprehending the world'; and according to phenomenological doctrine, this manner of apprehension can be described in abstraction from its object, though this would not be the complete account. The complete account of emotion must treat of the conjunction of subject and object, the 'indissoluble synthesis'. We see the world in a certain light, namely as making certain demands on us. Already it is clear that such a way of seeing cannot be described without reference both to the percipient, on whom the demand is made, and to the perceived object. But our ordinary life is not a matter of mere perception. We have things to get done, and we see things as means or as obstacles to this. We make a kind of map of the world for ourselves, a 'hodological' map, charting out the paths by which we have to reach our various goals, and in the light of this map we see the world before us as if it were an artefact of our own. But there are blocks and difficulties as well as routes, and when the obstacles become too great, we pretend that we can get what we need by magic instead of by the proper, natural, means. Now this effort to change the world by magical means, although it is essentially goal-directed, is not actually something upon which, at the time, we are in a position to reflect. It is not an object of consciousness. It is part of consciousness in the sense we have discussed; that is, it is an apprehension of the world, accompanied by the knowledge that we are apprehending the world in a certain way. Sartre claims that his account of the *change in the form in which we apprehend things* when cornered is intelligible in a way that Dembo's cannot be, since it starts with the concept of an emotion as a way of seeing the world about us, that is as cognitive. The new apprehension of the world produces new behaviour, but ineffectual and would-be-magical behaviour. We aim to change the world, but if we cannot do this we change ourselves. In extreme cases we may even faint, thus magically annihilating the world for ourselves by severing our connection with it for the time being.

Sartre, having expounded his general theory of the emotions, then sketches in various examples to show how they are to be interpreted in the light of the general explanation. It must be admitted that the account fits best those emotions which are one way or another distressing, such as anger or despair. It is less intelligible as an account of the agreeable emotions. For example, the account of the feeling of horror which we may experience on seeing a face at the window is entirely plausible. The concept of magic here has a double role. We feel terror because we are seeing the world, not rationally as a set of means and ends, nor as a collection of tools which we may use, or methods which may be employed for this or that purpose, but as 'one non-utilizable whole'. That is to say, the object of terror acts upon us immediately, and we do not use the normal categories of the possible and the impossible. Rationally, we might calculate that the window is shut, and the man outside could not get in, and that if he did he would not harm us, but none of this enters into the horrific vision of the face. It is as if it were not separated from us by any space, nor by any other physical objects which would in fact afford us protection. And since the face terrifies us as a magical object which is not bound by ordinary physical impossibilities, we attempt to combat the danger by magic too; not, that is, by taking rational steps to achieve our aim, but by screaming or fainting, to blot out the object of horror. 'The magical' is the name of one of the many ways we have of seeing the world. It is an inferior, more primitive way than the way of seeing which is normal to us in our practical life. So emotion is a kind of sinking into an inferior mode of consciousness, 'Emotion arises when the world of the utilizable vanishes abruptly, and the world of magic appears in its place.'

In conclusion, Sartre states that the theory which he has only sketched in this essay is both *a priori* and empirical; it starts from a concept of man as a being in the world, but a being of a certain kind with certain general potentialities; but it has recourse to experience and observation to show that this, that or the other emotion occurs and is of such and such a sort. He views his task, then, in propounding such a theory, as partly descriptive, and partly metaphysical. That is to say he is not concerned only to describe or even to define emotion, but to show that human beings are of such a kind that they must adopt the characteristic behaviour which he ascribes to them. But they cannot be treated in isolation. It is impossible for Sartre to propound a theory of human nature without taking into account the fact that human beings necessarily have some sort of cognitive relation to the world. The central existentialist doctrine is that men are nothing except what they choose to become, their essence consists in what they choose to do. But it also consists in what they choose to know, under what aspect they choose to see the world. Emotion arises when they choose to see the world in a particular way, namely the magical. It is an essential part of human nature to be capable of this. If this is the doctrine of the essay, it is easy to see how it forms an introduction, or an essential append-age, to *L'Etre et le Néant*, the purpose of which is precisely to enlarge upon the theme that people, being put down, as it were, in the world, choose their relation with it, both in the cognitive and the practical sphere. On a larger scale, and in more detail, we are given Sartre's systematic description of man's place in the universe. The assumption which lies behind the present work is that such a description is possible.

INTRODUCTION

Psychology, phenomenology and phenomenological psychology

Psychology is a discipline which claims to be positive; that is, it tries to draw upon the resources of experience alone. We are, of course, no longer in the days of the associationists, and contemporary psychologists do not forbid themselves to *interrogate* and to *interpret*. But they try to confront their subject as the physicist confronts his. We must however delimit this concept of experience when we speak of contemporary psychology, for there is, after all, a multitude of diverse experiences and we may, for example, have to decide whether an experience of essences or of values, or a religious experience, really exists or not. The psychologist tries to make use of only two well-defined types of experience: that which is given to us by spatiotemporal experience of organized bodies, and the intuitive knowledge of ourselves which we call reflective experience. When there are debates about method among psychologists they almost always bear upon the problem whether these two kinds of information are complementary. Ought one to be subordinated to the other? Or ought one of them to be resolutely disregarded? But there is agreement upon one essential principle: that their enquiries should begin first of all from the facts. And if we ask ourselves what is a fact, we see that it is defined in this way: that one must *meet* with it in the course of research, and that it is always presented as an unexpected enrichment and a novelty in relation to the antecedent facts. We must not then count upon the facts to organize themselves into a synthetic whole which would deliver its meaning by itself. In other words, if what we call anthropology is a discipline which seeks to define the essence of man and the human condition, then psychology – even the psychology of man – is not, and never will be an anthropology. It does not set out to define and limit *a priori* the object of its research. The notion of man that it accepts is quite empirical: all over the world there is a certain number of creatures that offer analogous characteristics. From other sciences, moreover, sociology and physiology, we have learned that certain objective relations exist between these creatures. No more is needed to justify the psychologist in accepting, prudently and as a working hypothesis, the provisional limitation of his researches to this group of creatures. The means of relevant information at our disposal are indeed more easily accessible since they live in society, possess languages and leave records. But the psychologist does not commit himself: he does not know whether the notion of man is arbitrary. It may be too *extensive*; there is nothing to show that the Australian primitive can be placed in the same psychological class as the American workman of 1939. Or it may be *too narrow*; nothing tells us that there is an abyss separating the higher apes from any human creature. In any case, the psychologist strictly is forbidden to consider the men around him as men *like himself*. That notion of likeness, upon which one could perhaps build up an anthropology, seems to him foolish and dangerous. He will gladly admit, with the reservations mentioned above, that he is *a* man – that is, that he belongs to this provisionally isolated class. But he will think that this human character should be conferred upon him *a posteriori*, and that he cannot, *qua* member of this class, be a privileged object of study, except for experimental convenience. He will learn then *from others* that he is a man: his human nature will not be revealed in any special manner under the pretext that he *is* himself that which he is studying. Introspection here, like 'objective' experimentation there, will furnish nothing but facts. If, later on, there ought to be a definitive concept of *man* – which itself is doubtful – this concept is to be envisaged only as the crowning concept of a completed science, which means that it is postponed to infinity. Nor would this be more than a unifying hypothesis invented in order to co-ordinate, hierarchically, the infinite collection of facts brought to light. Which means that the idea of man, if it ever acquires a positive meaning, will be only a conjecture intended to establish connections between the disparate materials and will derive its probability only from its success. Pierce defined the hypothesis as the sum of the experimental results which it enables us to predict. Thus the idea of man could only be the sum of the facts which it unifies. If, however, some psychologists made use of a certain conception of man *before* this ultimate synthesis was possible, it could be only on their personal

---

account and as a leading idea or, better, as an idea in the Kantian sense, and their primary duty would be never to forget that it was merely a regulative concept.

It follows from all these precautions that psychology, in so far as it claims to be a science, can furnish no more than a sum of heteroclite facts, the majority of which have no link between them. What could be more different, for instance, than the study of the stroboscopic illusion and the study of the inferiority complex? This disorder does not arise by chance, but from the very principles of the science of psychology. To wait upon the *fact* is, by definition, to wait upon the isolated; it is to prefer, positively, the accident to the essential, the contingent to the necessary, disorder to order. It is to discard, in principle, the essential as something in the future – 'that is for later on, when we have collected enough facts'. The psychologists do not notice, indeed, that it is just as impossible to attain the essence by heaping up the accidents as it is to arrive at unity by the indefinite addition of figures to the right of 0.99. If their only aim is to accumulate observations of detail there is nothing to be said, except that one can see little interest in the collectors' labours. But, if, in their modesty, they are animated by the hope, laudable in itself, that they will eventually realize an anthropological synthesis upon the basis of their monographs, then their aim is completely self-contradictory. They may say that this precisely is the method and the ambition of the natural sciences. To that we must reply that the aim of the sciences of nature is not to know *the world*, but the conditions under which certain general phenomena are possible. It is a good while since the notion of the *world* has succumbed under the criticisms of the methodologists, just because we cannot apply the methods of the positive sciences and at the same time expect them to lead us one day to a discovery of the meaning of the synthetic totality that we call the world. But *man* is a being of the same type as the *world*; it is even possible that, as Heidegger believes, the notions of the world and of 'human-reality' (*Dasein*) are inseparable. Precisely for that reason, psychology ought to resign itself to missing human-reality, if indeed that human-reality exists.

Applied to a particular example, to the study of the emotions for instance, what is to be gained from the principles and methods of the psychologist? First of all, our knowledge of emotion will be something additional to and *outside* all our other knowledge about psychic being. Emotion will present itself as an irreducible novelty in relation to the phenomena of attention, of memory, etc. You can indeed inspect these phenomena, and the empirical notions that the psychologists lead us to form about them, you can turn and turn them about as you will, but you will not find they have the slightest essential relation to emotion. However, the psychologist admits that man has emotions, he knows that from experience. In this view, emotion is primarily and in principle an *accident*. In treatises on psychology it is the subject of one chapter after the other chapters, much as in chemical treatises calcium might come after hydrogen and sulphur. As for studying the conditions under which an emotion is possible – enquiring, that is, whether the very structure of the human-reality renders the emotions possible and *how* it does so – to the psychologist this would seem needless and absurd. What is the use of enquiring whether emotion is possible, seeing that manifestly it *exists*? It is also to experience that the psychologist appeals in order to establish the limits of emotive phenomena and to define them. And, truth to tell, this may well awaken him to the fact that he already has an *idea* of emotion, for after examining the facts, he will draw a line of demarcation between the facts of emotion and those of a quite different order. How could experience supply him with a principle of demarcation if he did not already have one? But the psychologist prefers to hold fast to the belief that the facts fall into groups of themselves under his gaze.

The question now is how to *study* the emotions one has isolated. To this end, it is advisable to produce some emotional situations or turn our attention to the particularly emotional subjects offered to us by pathology. We will then try to determine the factors in such complex states: we will isolate the *bodily reactions* (which moreover we can establish with the greatest precision), the *behaviour* and the state of consciousness properly so called. After that, we shall be in a position to formulate our laws and put forward our explanations; that is, we shall try to relate these three types of factors in an irreversible order. If I am supporter of the intellectualist theory, for example, I shall set up a constant and irreversible succession between the interior state of consciousness considered as antecedent and the physiological disturbances considered as consequences. If, on the contrary, I agree with the advocates of the peripheric theory (that 'a mother is sad because she weeps'), I shall limit myself, fundamentally, to the reverse order of the factors. What is certain in any case is that I shall not look for the explanation or the laws of emotion in the general structure of the human-reality, but, on the contrary, in the development of the emotion itself; so that, even when duly described and explained, the emotion will never be more than one fact among others, a fact enclosed in itself, which will never enable anyone to understand anything else, nor to grasp by means of it the essential reality of man.

It was in reaction against the insufficiencies of psychology and of psychologism that there grew up, some thirty years ago, a new discipline, that of phenomenology. Its founder, Husserl, was first of all struck by this truth: that there is an incommensurability between essences and facts, and that whoever begins his researches with facts will never attain to essences. If I am looking for the psychic facts that underlie the arithmetical attitude of a man who is counting and calculating I shall never succeed in reconstituting the arithmetical essences of unity, of number and of numerical operations. Without, however, renouncing the idea of experience (the principle of phenomenology is to 'go to the things themselves', and its method is founded upon the eidetic intuition), it must at least be made more flexible; room must be made for the experiences of essences and values; we must even recognize that essences alone enable us to classify and examine facts. If we did not have implicit recourse to the essence of emotion it would be impossible for us to distinguish, among the multitude of psychic facts, this particular group of the facts of emotivity. Since, then, we have anyhow taken implicit recourse to the essence of emotion, phenomenology prescribes that we make our recourse explicit – that we should fix, once for all and by concepts, the content of this essence. It is easy to see that, for phenomenology, the notion of man can no longer be taken as an empirical concept derived from historical generalization; but that on the contrary we are obliged to make use, without saying so, of the *a priori* essence of the *human being* to give a fairly solid basis to the generalizations of the psychologist. Psychology, moreover, envisaged as the science of certain human facts, cannot be our starting-point, since the psychic facts that we meet with are never prior. They, in their essential structure, are reactions of man to the world: they therefore presuppose man and the world, and cannot take on their true meaning unless those two notions have first been elucidated. If we want to found a psychology we must go beyond the psychic, beyond the situation of man in the world, even to the very source of man, of the world and of the psychic; to the transcendental and constitutive consciousness that we attain through a 'phenomenological reduction', or 'putting the world in brackets'. It is this consciousness that must be interrogated; and what gives value to its answers is that it is *mine*. Husserl knows how to take advantage of that absolute proximity of consciousness to itself, which the psychologists do not choose to profit by. He takes advantage of it wittingly and with absolute confidence, because all consciousness exists precisely to the degree that it is consciousness of existing. But here, as above, he refuses to question consciousness about the *facts*, which would be to find the disorder of psychology again upon the transcendental plane. What he sets out to describe and to fix in concepts are precisely the essences which preside over developments in the transcendental field. Thus there will be, for instance, a phenomenology of emotion which, after 'putting the world in brackets', will study emotion as a purely transcendental phenomenon, not considering particular emotions, but seeking to attain and elucidate the transcendent essence of emotion as an organized type of consciousness.

The absolute proximity of the investigator to the object investigated is also the point of departure for another phenomenologist, Heidegger. What must differentiate all research into man from other types of strict investigation is precisely this privileged circumstance, that the human-reality is *ourselves*. 'The existent that we have to analyse,' writes

Heidegger, 'is ourselves. The being of this existent is my own.'[1]
And it is no negligible matter that this human-reality should
be myself, because it is precisely for the human reality that to
exist is always to assume its being; that is, to be responsible for
it instead of receiving it from outside, as a pebble does. And
since 'the human reality' is essentially its own possiblity, this
existent can itself 'choose' what it will be, achieve itself – or
lose itself.[2] 'This assumption' of itself which characterizes the
human reality implies an understanding of the human reality
by itself, however obscure an understanding this may be. 'In
the being of this existent, the latter relates itself to its being.'[3]
For indeed this understanding is not a quality that comes to
the human reality from without, but is its own mode of existence. Thus the human reality which is myself assumes its own
being by understanding it. This understanding is mine. I am,
then, first of all, a being who more or less obscurely understands his reality as a man, which means that I make myself a
man by understanding myself as such. I can therefore question myself and, on the basis of that interrogation, carry out
an analysis of the 'human reality' which will serve as the basis
for an anthropology. Here too, of course, the procedure is not
to be one of introspection; firstly, because introspection
meets with nothing but facts, and secondly, because my comprehension of the human reality is dim and inauthentic. It has
to be made explicit and corrected. In any case, the hermen-
eutic of existence will be sufficient foundation for an anthropology, and this anthropology will serve as a basis for all
psychology. We are thus taking up a position opposite to that

[1] *Sein und Zeit*, p. 41.
[2] Ibid, p. 41.
[3] Ibid, p. 43.

of the psychologists, since we *start* from the synthetic totality that man is, and establish the essence of man before beginning our psychology.

At all events, phenomenology is the study of phenomena – not of the facts. And by a phenomenon we are to understand 'that which announces itself', that of which the reality precisely is the appearance. And this 'announcement of itself' is not that of anything else . . . the being of the existent is not a thing 'behind which' there is still something else which 'does not yet appear'.[1] Indeed, for the human reality, to exist is, according to Heidegger, to assume its own being in an existential mode of understanding. And according to Husserl, to exist is, for consciousness, to appear to itself. Since the appearance here is the absolute, it is the appearance which has to be described and enquired into. From this point of view, Heidegger thinks that, in every human attitude – in emotion, for example, since we have been speaking of that – we can rediscover the whole of the human reality, for emotion is the human reality assuming itself and 'emotionally-directing' itself towards the world. Husserl, for his part, thinks that a phenomenological description of emotion will reveal the essential structures of consciousness, seeing that an emotion precisely is a consciousness. And reciprocally, a problem will arise that the psychologist does not even suspect: can one conceive of consciousnesses which do not include emotion among their potentialities or must we indeed regard it as an indispensable constituent of consciousness? Thus the phenomenologist will interrogate emotion *about consciousness* or *about man*; he will enquire not only what it is, but what it has to tell us about a being, one of whose characteristics is just this,

[1] *Sein und Zeit*, pp. 35–6

that it is capable of being moved. And conversely, he will interrogate consciousness, the human reality, about emotion: what must a consciousness be, that emotion should be possible, perhaps that it should even be necessary?

We are now able to understand why the psychologist distrusts phenomenology. The initial precaution of the psychologist is, in effect, to consider the psychic state from an aspect that will divest it of all *signification*. For him a psychic state is always a *fact* and, as such, always accidental. This accidental character is indeed what the psychologist most firmly maintains. If we ask of a scientist: why do bodies attract one another according to Newton's law? he will reply: I know nothing about that; because it is so. And if we ask him: what does that attraction signify? he will answer: it does not signify anything; it just is. Similarly, the psychologist, questioned about emotion, is quite proud to affirm: 'It exists. Why? I know nothing of that, I simply state the fact. I do not know its signification.' To the phenomenologist, on the other hand, every human fact is of its essence significant. If you deprive it of its significance you rob it of its nature as a human fact. The task of the phenomenologist, then, will be to study the significance of emotion. What are we to understand by that?

To signify is to indicate something else; and to indicate it in such a way that in developing the signification one finds precisely the thing signified. For the psychologist emotion signifies nothing, because he studies it as a fact; that is, by separating it from everything else. It will then be non-significant from the start; but if every human fact is in truth significant, this emotion of the psychologists is of its nature dead, non-psychic, inhuman. Whereas, if we want to see emotion as the phenomenologists see it, as a true phenomenon of consciousness, we shall have to consider it as significant first of all; and this means that we shall affirm that it is strictly to the degree that it signifies. We shall not begin by losing our way in the study of psychological facts, simply because, taken by themselves and in isolation, they signify *almost* nothing: they are, and that is all. On the contrary, we shall try, by developing the significance of behaviour and of disturbed consciousness, to explain what is signified. And what this is we know from the beginning: an emotion signifies *in its own manner* the whole of the consciousness, or, if we take our stand on the existential plane, of the human reality. It is not an accident, because the human reality is not a sum of facts; it expresses under a definite aspect the synthetic human entirety in its integrity. And by that we must in no wise be understood to mean that it is the effect of the human reality. It is that human reality itself, realizing itself in the form of 'emotion'. Hence it is impossible to regard emotion as a psycho-physiological disorder. It has its own essence, its peculiar structures, its laws of appearance, its meaning. It cannot possibly come from *outside* the human reality. It is man, on the contrary, who *assumes* his emotion, and emotion is therefore an organized form of human existence.

It is not our intention here to attempt a phenomenological study of emotion. Such a study, if we had one, would deal with affectivity as an existential mode of the human reality. But our ambition is more limited. We would rather try, in one defined and concrete case, that of emotion, to see whether pure psychology could derive a method and some instruction from phenomenology. We will not quarrel with psychology for not bringing man into question or putting the world in brackets. It takes man in the world as he presents himself in a multitude of situations: at the restaurant, in the family, at war. In a general way, what interests psychology is *man in situation*.

In itself it is, as we have seen, subordinate to phenomenology, since a truly positive study of man in situation would have first to have elucidated the notions of man, of the world, of being-in-the-world, and of situation. But, after all, phenomenology is hardly born as yet, and all these notions are very far from a definitive elucidation. Ought psychology to wait until phenomenology comes to maturity? We do not think so. But even if it does not wait for the definitive constitution of an anthropology, it should not forget that this anthropology is realisable, and that if one day it is realised, all the psychological disciplines will have to draw upon its resources. For the time being, psychology should endeavour not so much to collect the facts as to interrogate the *phenomena* – that is, the actual psychic events in so far as these are significations, not in so far as they are pure facts. For instance, it should recognize that emotion *does not exist*, considered as a physical phenomenon, for a body cannot be emotional, not being able to attribute a meaning to its own manifestations. Psychology will immediately look for something beyond the vascular or respiratory disturbances, this something beyond being the *meaning* of the joy or sadness. But since this meaning is precisely not a quality superposed from without upon the joy or the sadness, since it exists only to the degree that it appears – namely, to which it is *assumed* by the human-reality – it is the consciousness itself that is to be interrogated, for joy is joy only in so far as it appears as such. And, precisely because psychology is not looking for facts, but for their significations, it will abandon the method of inductive introspection or empirical external observation and seek only to grasp and to fix the essence of the phenomena. Psychology too will then offer itself as an eidetic science. Only, it will not be aiming, through study of the psychic phenomenon, at what is

___

13

ultimately *signified*, which is indeed the totality of man. It does not dispose of sufficient means to attempt that study. What will interest it, however, and this alone, is the phenomenon *inasmuch as it signifies*. Just so might I seek to grasp the essence of the proletariat through the word 'proletariat'. In that case I should be doing sociology. But the linguist studies the word 'proletariat' *in so far as it means proletariat* and will be worrying himself about the vicissitudes of the word as a transmitter of meaning.

Such a science is perfectly possible. What is lacking for it to become real? To have proved itself. We have seen that if the human-reality appears to the psychologist as a collection of heteroclite data, this is because the psychologist has voluntarily placed himself upon the terrain where the human-reality must look to him like that. But this does not necessarily imply that the human reality is anything else but a collection. What we have proved is only that it *cannot* appear otherwise to the psychologist. We have yet to see whether it will bear, to the depths, a phenomenological investigation – whether emotion, for instance, is in truth a phenomenon that signifies. To come clear about this, there is only one way; that which, moreover, the phenomenologist himself recommends: to 'go to the things themselves'. May the following pages be regarded as an *experiment* in phenomenological psychology. We shall try to place ourselves upon the terrain of signification, and to treat emotion as a *phenomenon*.

SKETCH FOR A THEORY OF
THE EMOTIONS

I. THE CLASSIC THEORIES

We all know the criticisms that have been urged against the peripheric theory of the emotions. How can it explain the subtler emotions? Or passive enjoyment? How can we admit that ordinary organic reactions suffice to render an account of distinct psychic states? How can quantitative and, by the same token, quasicontinuous modifications in the vegetative functions correspond to a qualitative series of states irreducible to one another? For example, the physiological modifications which correspond to anger differ only by their intensity from those that accompany joy (somewhat quicker respiratory rhythm, slight augmentation of muscular tone, increase of biochemical exchanges, of arterial tension, etc.). For all that, anger is not a greater intensity of joy; it is something else, at least as it presents itself to consciousness. It would be useless to show that there is an excitation in joy which predisposes to anger, citing the cases of lunatics who are constantly passing from joy to anger (for instance, by rocking to and fro on a seat at an accelerating rhythm). The idiot who has become angry is not 'ultra-joyful'. Even if he has *passed* from joy to anger (and there is nothing to justify our affirming that there has not been a number of psychic events meanwhile) anger is irreducible to joy.

It seems to me that the basis common to all these objections might be summarized thus: William James distinguishes in emotion two groups of phenomena; a group of physiological phenomena and a group of psychological phenomena which we shall call, as he does, the *state* of consciousness. The essence of his thesis is that the states of consciousness called joy, anger and so forth are nothing but the consciousness of physiological manifestations – or, if you will, their projection into consciousness. Now, of all the critics of James who have successively examined the 'state' of consciousness, 'emotion' and the accompanying physiological manifestations, not one *recognizes* the former as being the projection of, or the shadow cast by, the latter. They find *more* in it, and – whether they are clearly conscious of this or not – *something else*. *More*; for whatever extravagance we may ascribe, in imagination, to the disorder of the body, we still fail to understand why the corresponding consciousness should be, for instance, a *terrorized* consciousness. Terror is an extremely painful, even unbearable state, and it is inconceivable that a bodily condition, taken for itself and in itself, could appear in consciousness with this atrocious character. *Something else*; for, in effect, and even if the emotion objectively perceived presented itself as a physiological disorder, as a fact of consciousness it is neither disorder nor chaos pure and simple, it has a meaning, it signifies something. And by this we do not only mean that it is presented as a pure quality. It arises as a certain relation between our psychic being and the world; and this relation – or rather our awareness of it – is not a chaotic relationship between the self and the universe; it is an organized and describable structure.

I cannot see that the corticothalamic sensitivity, recently invented by the same people who made these criticisms of James, provides a satisfactory answer to the question. First of all, the peripheric theory of James had one big advantage: it took account only of physiological disturbances directly or indirectly discernible. The theory of cerebral sensibility appeals to a cortical disturbance that is unverifiable. Sherrington made some experiments on dogs, and one can certainly praise his operational dexterity. But these experiments taken by themselves prove *absolutely* nothing. Simply because the head of a dog practically isolated from its body still gives signs of emotion, I cannot see that we have the right to conclude that the *dog* is feeling a complete emotion. Besides, even supposing that the existence of a corticothalamic sensitivity were established, it would still be necessary to ask the previous question: can a physiological disturbance, *whatever it may be*, render an account of the *organized* character of an emotion?

That is what Janet very well understood, but expressed without much felicity when he said that James, in his description of emotion, had left out the psychic. Basing himself exclusively upon objective grounds, Janet wants to register only the external manifestations of emotion. But, even considering none but the organic phenomena that can be described and disclosed from the outside, he thinks that these phenomena are immediately susceptible of being classified under two categories: the psychic phenomena, or behaviour, and the physiological phenomena. A theory of emotion which sought to restore the preponderant part played by the psyche would have to treat emotion as a kind of behaviour. Yet for all that, Janet is aware no less than James of the apparent disorder presented by every emotion. He therefore treats emotion as a behaviour that is less well adapted, or, if one prefers, a behaviour of disadaptation, a behaviour of defeat. When the task is too difficult and we cannot maintain the higher behaviour appropriate to it, the psychic energy that has been released takes another path; we adopt an inferior behaviour which necessitates a lesser psychic tension. Here, for instance, is a girl whose father has just told her that he has pains in the arms, and that he has some fear of paralysis. She falls to the ground, prey to a violent emotion which returns a few days later with the same violence, and which finally obliges her to seek help from doctors. In the course of her treatment she confesses that the thought of nursing her father, and leading the austere life of a nurse, had suddenly appeared to her as insupportable. Here, then, the emotion represents an attitude of defeat; it is the substitute for the 'non-maintainable-conduct-of-a-nurse'. Similarly, in his work on *Obsession and Psychasthenia*, Janet cites the cases of several patients who, having come to make confessions to him, could not finish their confessions, but broke down in tears, sometimes even bringing on a nervous crisis. Here again, the required behaviour is too difficult. The weeping, or the nervous crisis, represents a behaviour of defeat, which substitutes itself for the former by a diversion. The point needs no elaboration; examples are abundant. Who does not remember having engaged in exchanges of raillery with a comrade, and remaining calm so long as the competition seemed equal, but becoming irritated as soon as one found oneself with nothing more to say?

Thus Janet could pride himself upon having reintegrated the psyche with the emotions: the consciousness that we have of emotion – a consciousness which, moreover, is here only a secondary phenomenon[1] – is no longer simply the correlative of physiological disturbances: it is the awareness of a defeat and is a behaviour of defeat. The theory looks attractive: it is indeed a *psychological* thesis, and yet it is of a quite mechanistic simplicity. The phenomenon of diversion is nothing more than a switching of the liberated nervous energy on to another line.

And yet, how many obscurities there are in these few notions which at first look so clear! Upon better consideration of the case, if Janet manages to improve upon James it is only by making use, implicitly, of a finality which his theory explicitly repudiates. What in fact is a 'behaviour of defeat'? Are we simply to understand by this, an automatic substitute for the superior line of conduct that we cannot pursue? In that case the nervous energy would be discharged at hazard according to the law of the least resistance. But then the emotive reactions would be less like a behaviour of defeat than a lack of behaviour. Instead of an adapted reaction there would be a diffuse organic reaction – a disorder. But is not that just what James is saying? Does not the emotion, in his view, intervene precisely at the moment of the breakdown of an adaptation, and does it not consist essentially of the sum of the disorders that this non-adaptation entails for the organism? No doubt Janet puts the emphasis more than James does upon the *defeat*. But what are we to understand by it? If we

---

[1] But not an epiphenomenon: consciousness is behaviour of behaviours.

regard the individual objectively as a system of behaviour, and if the deviation takes place automatically, then there is no defeat, it does not exist; all that happens is the replacement of one kind of behaviour by a diffuse set of organic manifestations. If emotion is to have the psychic significance of defeat, consciousness must intervene and confer that signification upon it, there must be a conscious retention of the superior conduct as a possibility and a consciousness of the emotion as a defeat precisely in relation to that superior behaviour. But that would be to give consciousness a constitutive function, which Janet will not have at any price. If one wanted to preserve a meaning in Janet's theory, one would be logically obliged to adopt the position of M. Wallon who, in his article in the *Revue des Cours et Conférences*, puts forward the following interpretation: In the infant, there is a primitive nerve circuit. All the reactions of a new-born child, to tickling, pain and so on (shiverings, diffused muscular contractions, acceleration of the cardiac rhythm, etc.), are under the control of this circuit, and would thus constitute a primary organic adaptation – an inherited adaptation, of course. Later on, we learn how to behave, and set up new patterns of reaction – that is, new circuits. But when, in a new and difficult situation, we cannot produce adapted behaviour appropriate to it we fall back upon the primitive nervous circuit. We can see that this theory represents a transposition of Janet's view into the sphere of pure behaviourism; for what it amounts to is that the emotional reactions are not seen as a mere disorder, but as a lesser adaptation: the first organized system of defensive reflexes – that of the infant's nerve-circuit – is ill-adapted to cope with the needs of the adult; but in itself it is a functional organisation, analogous to the respiratory reflex, for instance. But we can also see that this thesis differs from that of James only upon the presupposition of an organic unity linking all the emotive manifestations together. It goes without saying that James would have accepted the existence of such a circuit without embarrassment if it had been proved. He would then have held that this modification of his own theory was of little importance because it was of a purely physiological order. Janet, therefore, if we hold him strictly to the terms of his thesis, is much closer to James than he would have cared to say. He has failed in his attempt to reintroduce the 'psychic' into emotion, nor has he explained why there are *various* kinds of behaviour in defeat; why I may react to a sudden aggression by fear or by anger. The cases he recounts, moreover, are almost all reducible to emotional perturbations not very different from one another (tears, nervous attacks, etc.), much nearer to emotional shock properly so called than to emotion as such.

But in Janet's work there seems to be an underlying theory of emotion – and also of behaviour in general – which would reintroduce finality without mentioning it. In his general expositions concerning psychasthenia or affectivity he insists, as we have said, upon the automatic character of the diversion, but in many of his descriptions he gives us to understand that the patient falls back upon the inferior behaviour in *order not to* maintain the superior behaviour. Here, it is the patient himself who proclaims his defeat even before he engages in the struggle, and the emotional behaviour supervenes *to mask* his inability to pursue the line of adapted behaviour. Let us return to the example we were citing above: the patient who comes to see Janet wants to entrust him with the secret of her troubles and a minute description of her obsessions. But she cannot: this is social behaviour that is too difficult for her. *Then* she bursts into tears. But is she weeping *because* she can say nothing? Is her sobbing a vain effort to do so, a diffuse upheaval that represents the decomposition of the behaviour she has found too difficult? Or rather, is she not crying precisely in order *not* to say anything? Between these two interpretations the difference may seem small at first sight: by both hypotheses a course of behaviour proves impossible to maintain, and according to either there is a replacement of this behaviour by diffuse manifestations. Besides, Janet passes freely from the one to the other; that is what makes his theory ambiguous. For in reality there is an abyss of difference between the two interpretations. The former is, in effect, purely mechanistic and – as we have seen – is at bottom fairly close to James's views. The latter, on the other hand, really introduces something new: it alone truly deserves the name of a psychological theory of the emotions; it alone treats emotion as a way of behaving. For, indeed, if we are here reintroducing finality, we can well conceive that emotional behaviour is not a disorder at all; that it is an organized pattern of means directed to an end. And these means are *summoned up* in order to mask, replace or reject a line of conduct that one cannot or will not pursue. At the same time, the explanation of the diversity of emotions becomes easy: they represent, each one of them, a different way of eluding a difficulty, a particular way of escape, a special trick.

But Janet has given us what he could: he is too uncertain, divided between a finality that is spontaneous and a mechanism on principle. It is not to him that we look for an exposition of this pure theory of emotional behaviour. We find it in outline among the disciples of Kohler and notably in Lewin[1] and Dembo.[2] Here is what P. Guillaume writes upon this subject in his *Psychologie de la Forme:*[3]

SKETCH FOR A THEORY OF THE EMOTIONS

'Let us take the simplest example: we ask a subject to reach for an object placed upon a chair, but without putting a foot outside a circle traced upon the ground: the distances are so calculated as to make the act very difficult or impossible by direct means, but the problem can be resolved by indirect means. . . . Here, the force directed towards the object takes on a clear, concrete meaning. On the other hand, these problems present an obstacle to the direct execution of the action, an obstacle that may be either material or moral – for instance, a rule one has undertaken to observe. Thus, in our example, the circle that one must not overstep presents, to the perception of the subject, a barrier – from which there emanates a force directly in opposition to the former. The conflict between the two forces sets up a tension in the phenomenal field. If the solution is found, the successful action puts an end to the tension. . . . There is a whole psychology of the act of replacement or substitution, of the *ersatz* to which the school of Lewin has made an interesting contribution. Its form is very variable; the partial results achieved may help to fix it. Sometimes the subject facilitates the act by freeing himself from some of the imposed conditions of quantity, quality, speed or duration, and even by modifying the nature of his task; in other cases he performs unreal, symbolic actions; one makes an obviously useless gesture in the direction of the act; another describes the action instead of performing it, or imagines chimerical, fictive procedures (if only I had . . . one would

[1] Lewin, *Vorsatz, Wille und Bedurtnis*, Psy. Forschung, VII, 1926.
[2] Dembo, *Das Aerger als dynamisches Problem*. Psy. Forschung, 1931, pp. 1–144.
[3] (Bib. de Philosophie Scientifique), pp. 138–42.

need ...) outside the real or imposed conditions for its accomplishment. If acts of substitution are impossible, or do not produce an adequate solution, the tension persists, manifested by a tendency to abandon the problem, to wander away, or to withdraw into one's own thoughts in an attitude of passivity. As we have said, indeed, the subject finds himself subjected to the positive attraction of the end in view and to the negative, repellent influence of the barrier: furthermore, the fact that he has consented to undergo the trial has conferred a negative value upon all the other objects in the field, in the sense that all diversions irrelevant to the task are *ipso facto* impossible. The subject is thus imprisoned, as it were, in a space fenced in on every side: there is only one positive way out, and that is closed by the specific barrier. This situation corresponds to the diagram below:

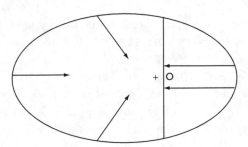

Escape is a merely barbarous solution, for it means breaking through the barrier and accepting a diminution of the self. Falling back upon one's self (encystment) which erects a protective barrier between the hostile field of action and oneself, is another, equally mediocre solution.

Prolongation of the ordeal may end in emotional disorders, or in other and still more primitive ways of liberating tensions. The fits of anger, sometimes very violent, which supervene in certain persons have been capably studied in the work of T. Dembo. The situation undergoes a structural simplification. In anger, and doubtless in all the emotions, there is a weakening of the barriers that separate the deeper from the more superficial levels of the self which normally ensure the regulation of action by the deep personality and maintain the self-control: a weakening of the barriers between the real and the unreal. On the other hand, because the path to action is blocked, tensions between the external and the internal continue to augment: a negative character extends uniformly to all the objects in the field, they lose their proper value. . . . The privileged way towards the goal having vanished, the differentiated structure that the problem had imposed upon the field is destroyed. The particular facts, notably the various physiological reactions which we are pleased to describe by attaching part-icular meanings to them, are not intelligible unless we start from this integral conception of the topology of emo-tion . . .'

Here, then, at the end of this long quotation, we arrive at a functional conception of anger. Clearly anger is not an instinct nor a habit, nor is it a calculated action; it is an abrupt solu-tion of conflict, a way of cutting the gordian knot. And we are back again at Janet's distinction between the superior kind of behaviour and the inferior or derived. But here that distinc-tion assumes its full meaning: it is we who put ourselves into a state of total inferiority, because at that very low level our demands are smaller; we satisfy ourselves at less cost. Being unable, in a state of high tension, to find the delicate and precise answer to a problem, we act upon ourselves, we abase and transform ourselves into a being for whom the grossest and least adapted solutions are good enough (for example, tearing up the paper on which a problem is stated). Thus anger now appears as an escape; the angry subject is like a man who is unable to untie the knots of the cords that bind him, and who writhes about in his bonds. And the 'angry' conduct, though less well adapted to the problem than the superior – and impossible – behaviour that would solve it, is still precisely and perfectly adapted to his need to break the tension, to shake the leaden weight off his shoulders. We shall be better able to understand the examples we were citing above: the psychasthenic who comes to see Janet wants to make her confession to him. But the task is too difficult. Here she is, in a confined, threatening world which is waiting for her to perform a definite action and at the same time repelling her. Janet himself signifies by his attitude that he is listening and is attentive; but at the same time his prestige, his personality, etc. repulse that confession. Escape she must from the unbearable tension! And the patient can do so only by exaggerating her weakness and her disarray, by distracting his attention from the task in hand and turning it upon herself (how unhappy I am!). Her own demeanour will transform Janet from her judge into her comforter by exteriorising and 'playing up' the very impossibility she finds in speaking, by commuting the precise need to give such and such information into a heavy, undifferentiated pressure of the whole world upon her. It is then that the sobbing and the nervous crisis ensue.

Similarly it is easy to understand the fit of anger that seizes me when I can think of nothing more to reply to a mocker. Here anger does not play quite the same part as in the example given by Dembo. My need is to switch the discussion on to another plane. I have not been witty enough, so become formidable and intimidating. I want to arouse fear the same time I make use of inferior alternatives (*ersatze* vanquish my adversary – insults, threats which have to 'do instead of' the shaft of wit I failed to think of; for the abrupt change of attitude that I impose upon myself makes me less exacting about the choice of means.

And yet, at the point we have come to, we still feel unsatisfied. The emotional behaviour theory is perfect, but in its purity and perfection we can see its insufficiency. In all the examples we have quoted, the functional part played by emotion is indubitable. But as it stands, it is also incomprehensible. I mean that, for Dembo and the Gestalt psychologists, the passage from the state of seeking to the state of anger is explained as the break-up of one form and the reconstitution of another. And I can understand, if need be, the break-up of the form 'problem without solution'; but how can I admit the appearance of the other form? We must suppose that it presents itself clearly as the substitute for the previous form. It exists only in relation to this. We have, then, a single process – a transformation of form. But I cannot comprehend this transformation without first positing consciousness. Consciousness alone, by its synthetic activity, can break up and reconstitute forms without ceasing. It alone can account for the finality of emotion. Moreover, we have seen that the whole of the description of anger given by Guillaume according to Dembo shows that its aim is to transform the aspect of the world. It serves to 'weaken the barriers between the real and the unreal', to 'destroy the differentiated structure that the problem has imposed upon the world'. Admirable! but as soon as it is a question of positing a relation of the world to the self, we can no longer content ourselves with a psychology of form. It is quite clear that we must have recourse to the consciousness. And besides, is it not to consciousness, after all, that Guillaume is referring when he says that the angry subject 'weakens the barriers that separate the deeper from the more superficial levels of the self'? Thus the physiological theory of James has led us, by its own insufficiency, to Janet's theory of behaviour, the latter to the theory of functional emotion in form-psychology, and this refers us at last to the consciousness. That is where we ought to have begun, and it is now high time for us to formulate the real problem.

II. THE PSYCHOANALYTIC THEORY

We cannot understand an emotion unless we look for its signification. And this, by its nature, is of a functional order. We are therefore led to speak of a finality of emotion. This finality we can grasp very concretely by the objective examination of emotional behaviour. Here there is no question at all of a more or less obscure theory about emotion-instinct based upon a priori principles or postulates. Simple consideration of the facts brings us to an empirical intuition of the finalist meaning of emotion. If we try on the other hand to fix, in a complete intuition, the essence of emotion as an interpsychological fact, we see that this finality is inherent in its structure. And all the psychologists who have reflected upon the peripheric pheric theory of James have been more or less aware of this finalistic signification – this is what Janet, for instance, decorates with the name of 'psychic'; it is this that psychologists or physiologists like Cannon and Sherrington try to reintroduce into their descriptions of the emotional facts with their hypothesis of a cerebral sensibility; it is this, again, that we find in Wallon or, more recently, among the Gestalt psychologists. This finality presupposes a synthetic organization of behaviour which could only be the 'unconscious' of psychoanalysis, or consciousness. And it would be easy enough, if need be, to produce a psychoanalytic theory of emotional finality. One could show, without great difficulty, that anger or fear are means employed by unconscious urges to achieve symbolic satisfaction, to break out of a state of unbearable tension. One could thus account for this essential characteristic of emotion – that it is 'suffered', that it surprises, develops of itself according to its own laws, and that conscious efforts cannot modify its course to any very appreciable extent. This dissociation between the organized character of emotion – the organizing theme being relegated to the unconscious – and its ineluctable character, which it would not have for the consciousness of the subject, would render something like the same service in the psychological domain as the Kantian distinction between the empirical and the noumenal does in the domain of metaphysic.

It is certainly true that psychoanalysis was the first to lay the emphasis upon the signification of psychic facts: that is, it was the first to insist upon the fact that every state of consciousness stands for something other than itself. For example: this clumsy theft perpetrated by a sexual-obsessive is not simply a clumsy theft. It refers to something else from the moment that we begin to consider it in the psychoanalyst's way as a phenomenon of self-punishment. Then it refers to the primary complex for which the patient is seeking to justify himself through self-punishment. We can see that a psychoanalytic theory of the emotions would be possible. Does it not already exist? There is that woman with a phobia for laurel. If she sees a clump of laurels, she faints. The psychoanalyst discovers that in her childhood there was a painful sexual incident associated with laurel bushes. What will be the corresponding emotion? A phenomenon of refusal, and of censorship. Not refusal of the laurel itself, but a refusal to relive the memory connected with laurels. Here the emotion is a flight from the revelation to follow, as sleep is sometimes a flight from a decision to be taken, and as the illnesses of certain young women are, according to Stekel, a flight from marriage. Naturally, emotion is not always an escape. We already have indications from the psychoanalysts of an interpretation of anger as a symbolic gratification of sexual tendencies. And certainly, none of these interpretations is to be thrust aside. That anger can signify sadism is in no doubt at all. That fainting away from passive fear signifies flight, the quest of a refuge, is also certain, and we shall try to show the reason for it. What is in question here is the principle itself of psychoanalytic explanation – that is what we want to consider here.

The psychoanalytic interpretation conceives the conscious phenomenon as the symbolic realization of a desire repressed by the censor. Note that, for consciousness, the desire is not involved in its symbolic realization. In so far as it exists by and in our consciousness it is only what it gives itself out to be: emotion, desire for sleep, theft, laurel-phobia, etc. If it were otherwise, if we had any consciousness, even only implicit, of the real desire, we should be in bad faith, and that is not what the psychoanalyst means. It follows that the signification of our conscious behaviour lies wholly outside that behaviour itself or, if one prefers it so, what is signified is entirely cut off from the signifier. This behaviour of the subject is, in itself, just what it is (if by 'in itself' we mean for itself), but it can be deciphered by the appropriate techniques as one would decipher a given language. In a word, the conscious fact is related to what it signifies, as a thing which is the *effect* of a certain event is related to that event: as, for example, the ashes of a fire extinct upon a mountain are related to the human beings who lit the fire. Their presence is not *contained* in the remaining cinders, but connected with them by a relation of causality: the relation is *external*, the ashes of the fire are *passive* considered in that causal relation, as every effect is in relation to its cause. A consciousness which had not acquired the necessary technical knowledge could not grasp these remains as *signs*. At the same time, the remains are what they are; that is, they exist in themselves, irrespective of all significant interpretation: they *are* fragments of half-burnt wood, and that is all.

Can we admit that a fact of consciousness could be like a thing in relation to its signification – that is, receive its meaning from outside like an external quality – as, for instance, this having been burnt by men who wanted to warm themselves is a quality external to the burnt wood? It would seem, first and foremost, that the effect of such an interpretation is to make consciousness into a thing in relation to what is signified: it is to admit that consciousness can constitute itself into a meaning without being aware of the meaning that it constitutes. There is a flagrant contradiction in this, unless we are to regard consciousness as an existent of the same type as a stone, or a pond. But in that case we must finally give up the Cartesian *cogito* and treat consciousness as a secondary and passive phenomenon. In so far as a consciousness *makes itself* it is never anything other than what it appears to be. If, then, it has a signification, it must contain this within itself as a structure of consciousness. This does not mean that the signification must be perfectly explicit. There are many possible degrees of condensation and of clarity. It only means that we should not interrogate the consciousness from outside, as one would study the remains of the fire or the encampment, but from within; that we should look into it for the signification. The consciousness, if the *cogito* is to be possible, is itself the *fact*, the *signification* and what is *signified*.

Truth to tell, what makes an exhaustive refutation of psychoanalysis so difficult is that the psychoanalyst himself does not regard the signification as conferred entirely from outside the consciousness. For him, there is always an internal analogy between the conscious fact and the desire it expresses, since the *conscious fact is symbolical of the expressed complex*. And for the psychoanalyst this symbolic character is obviously not external to the fact itself, but is *constitutive* of it. Upon this point we are in full agreement with him. That the symbolization is constitutive of the symbolic consciousness can be in no doubt whatever to anyone who believes in the absolute value of the Cartesian *cogito*. But this needs to be rightly understood: if symbolization is constitutive it is legitimate to see an immanent bond of *comprehension* between the symbolization and the symbol. Only, we must agree upon this, that consciousness *constitutes itself* by symbolization. In that case there is nothing behind it, and the relation between symbol, symbolized and symbolization is an intra-structural bond of consciousness. But if we go on to say that the consciousness is symbolizing under the causal compulsion of a transcendent fact — which is the repressed desire — we are falling back upon the theory previously indicated, which treats the relation of the signified to the signifying as a causal relation. The profound contradiction in all psychoanalysis is that it presents *at the same time* a bond of causality and a bond of understanding between the phenomena that it studies. These two types of relationship are incompatible. The theorist of psychoanalysis also establishes transcendent relations of rigid causality between the facts under observation (a pincushion in a dream always *signifies* a woman's breasts, entry into a carriage signifies the sexual act), whilst the practitioner assures himself of success by studying; that is, by flexible research into the intra-conscious relation between symbolization and symbol.

For our part, we do not reject the findings of psychoanalysis when they are obtained by the understanding. We limit ourselves to the denial that there is any value or intelligibility in its underlying theory of psychic causality. And moreover we affirm that, in so far as the psychoanalyst is making use of *understanding* to interpret consciousness, it would be better to recognize frankly that whatever is going on in consciousness can receive its explanation nowhere but from consciousness itself. And here we are brought back to our own point of departure: a theory of consciousness which attributes meaningful character to the emotive facts must look for that meaning in the consciousness itself. In other words, it is the consciousness which *makes itself* conscious, moved by the inner need for an inner signification.

And indeed, the advocates of psychoanalysis are at the same time raising a difficulty of principle. If consciousness organizes emotion as a special type of response adapted to an external situation, how does it manage to have no consciousness of this adaptation? And it must be granted that their theory renders a perfect account of this discrepancy between the signification and the consciousness – which need not astonish us since that is just what it was made for. Better still, they will say, in the majority of cases we are struggling, in our conscious spontaneity, against the development of emotional manifestations; we are trying to master our fear, to calm our anger, to restrain our weeping. Thus we have not only no consciousness of any finality of emotion, we are also rejecting emotion with all our strength and it invades us in spite of ourselves. A phenomenological description of emotion ought to resolve these contradictions.

III. OUTLINE OF A PHENOMENOLOGICAL THEORY

Perhaps it will assist us in our research to make a preliminary observation, one which might serve towards a general criticism of all the theories of emotion we have encountered (with the possible exception of Dembo's). For the majority of psychologists everything happens as though the consciousness of emotion were primarily a reflective consciousness; that is, as if the primary form of emotion, as a fact of consciousness, were its appearance to us as a modification of our psychic being – or, to use ordinary language, its being grasped first of all, as a *state of mind*. And certainly, it is always possible to become aware of emotion as a fact of consciousness, as when we say: I am angry, I am afraid, etc. But the fear does not begin as consciousness of being afraid, any more than the perception of this book is consciousness of perceiving it. The emotional consciousness is at first non-reflective, and upon that plane it cannot be consciousness of itself, except in the non-positional mode. The emotional consciousness is primarily consciousness of the world. There is no need to call to mind the whole theory of consciousness in order to understand this principle clearly. A few simple observations will suffice, and it is remarkable that the psychologists of emotion have never thought of making them. It is obvious indeed that the man who is frightened is afraid of something. Even if it is a case of one of those indefinite anxieties that one feels in the dark, in a sinister and deserted alley, etc., it is still of certain aspects of the night, or of the world, that one is afraid. And without doubt, all the psychologists have noted that emotion is touched off by some perception – a representative signal, etc. But for them, as it appears, emotion then parts company with the object to become absorbed in itself. Little reflection is needed to discover that, on the contrary, emotion returns to the object every moment and feeds upon it. They describe flight in fear, for instance, as though the flight were not first and foremost a flight from a certain object, as though that object did not remain constantly in the act of flight as its theme, the reason for it, as what one is *fleeing from*. And how can we speak about anger, in which one strikes, reviles and threatens, without mentioning the person who represents the objective unity of all those insults, menaces and blows? In a word, the emotional subject and the object of the emotion are united in an indissoluble synthesis. Emotion is a specific manner of apprehending the world. That is what Dembo alone has a glimpse of, although he does not give a reason for it. The subject who is seeking the solution of a practical problem is outside in the world, he is aware of the world at every moment throughout all his actions. If he fails in his attempt and grows irritated, the irritation itself is still a way in which the world appears to him. And it is not necessary that the subject, between his failure in action and his anger, should turn back upon himself and interpose a reflective consciousness. There may be continuous passage from the non-reflective consciousness 'instrumental world' (action) to the non-reflective consciousness 'hateful world' (anger). The latter is a transformation of the former.

35

For a better understanding of what is to follow, the reader will need to recall to mind the essence of *unreflecting behaviour*. We tend too easily to believe that action involves a constant passing from the non-reflective to the reflective, from the world to oneself. That is, that we grasp the problem (non-reflective consciousness of the world), then we see ourselves as having the problem to resolve (reflection); and that then, starting from that reflection, we conceive an action in so far as it has to be performed *by us* (reflection) after which we go down again into the world to perform the action (non-reflectively) now thinking only of the object acted upon. Thereafter, any new difficulties, any partial failures that require re-adjustment of means, send us back to the plane of reflection. According to this view, a constant movement inward and outward is constitutive of action.

Now it is certain that we can reflect upon our activity. But an operation *upon* the universe is generally executed without our having to leave the nonreflective plane. For example, at this moment I am writing, but I am not conscious of writing. Will someone say that habit has rendered me unconscious of the movements made by my hand in tracing the letters? That would be absurd. I may have the habit of writing, but not at all that of writing *such* words in *such* an order. In a general way, one should always distrust habit as an explanation. In reality, the act of writing is not at all unconscious, it is an actual structure of my consciousness. Only it is not conscious of itself. To write is to maintain an active awareness *of the words* as they come to birth under my pen. Not of the words inasmuch as they are written *by me*: I apprehend the words intuitively inasmuch as they have that structural quality, that they emerge *ex nihilo* and yet do not create themselves, that they are passively created. At the actual moment when I write a word,

I am not paying attention individually to each pothook formed under my hand. I am in a special state of attention, creative attention; I wait for the word – which I know in advance – to employ the hand that is writing and the pothooks it is tracing, and thus to realize itself.

And certainly, I am not conscious of the words in the same way as when I read what another person is writing, by looking over his shoulder. But that does not mean that I am conscious of myself as writing. The essential differences are these: first, that my intuitive understanding of what my neighbour is writing is of the type of 'probable evidence'. I grasp the words traced by his hand some time before he has traced them completely. But at the moment when, reading 'indep . . .', I intuitively seize upon the word 'independent', this word 'independent' presents itself as a probable reality, like the table or the chair. On the other hand, my intuitive grasp of the words that I myself am writing delivers them to me as certainties. The certitude in this case is a little peculiar: for it is not certain that the word 'certitude' which I am in the act of writing will appear (I may go crazy, change my mind, etc.), but it is certain that, if it does appear, it will appear as such. Thus the activity constitutes a succession of certain objects in a probable world; or let us say, if you will, that they are probable considered as future realities, but certain as potentialities of the world. Secondly, the words written by my neighbour make no demands on me; I contemplate them as they appear in succession as I might look at a table or a suitcase. The words that I am writing, on the contrary, are *exigent*. It is the precise manner in which I grasp them in the course of my creative activity that makes them what they are: they are potentialities that *have to be realized*. Not that have to be realized *by me*. The self does not appear at all in this. I simply feel the pull they exert; I feel their exigence objectively. I see them realizing themselves and, at the same time, demanding further realization. I can very well think that the words my neighbour is writing demand their realization from him, but I do not feel that demand. On the contrary the exigence of the words that I am tracing is directly present, weighty and felt. They impel and direct my hand. But not as though little demons, alive and active, were driving and guiding it in fact: this is a passive exigence. As for my hand, I am conscious of it in the sense that I see it before me as the instrument whereby the words realize themselves: it is an object in the world, but one that is at the same time present and lived. Here, for a moment, I hesitate: shall I write 'then' or 'consequently'? This does not in the least imply that I am falling back upon myself; but simply that the two possibilities 'then' and 'consequently' – but only as possibilities – appear, and enter into conflict.

We shall try elsewhere to describe the world one acts upon. What is important here is only to show that activity, as spontaneous, unreflecting consciousness, constitutes a certain existential stratum in the world, and that in order to act, there is no need to be conscious of oneself as acting – quite the contrary. In a word, unreflective conduct is not unconscious conduct. It is non-thetically conscious of self; and its way of being conscious of self is to transcend and apprehend itself out in the world as a quality of things. In this way we can understand all those exigences and those tensions of the world around us; in this way we can draw up a 'hodological'[1] chart of our Umwelt, a chart that will vary in function with our actions and our needs. Only, in a normal and well-adapted

---

[1] The expression is Lewin's.

activity the objects 'to be realised' present themselves as need-ing to be realized in specific ways. The means themselves appear to us as potentialities that lay claim to existence. This apprehension of the means as the one possible path to the attainment of the end (or, if there are n means, as the n that alone are possible) may be called the pragmatic intuition of the determinism of the world. From this point of view, the world around us — that which the Germans call the *Umwelt* — the world of our desires, our needs and of our activities, appears to be all furrowed with strait and narrow paths lead-ing to such and such determinate end, that is the appearance of a created object. Naturally, here and there, and to some extent everywhere, there are pitfalls and traps. One might compare this world to one of those pin-tables where for a penny in the slot you can set the little balls rolling: there are pathways traced between hedges of pins, and holes pierced where the pathways cross one another. The ball is required to complete a predetermined course, making use of the required paths and without dropping into the holes. This world is difficult. The notion of difficulty here is not a reflexive notion which would imply a relation to oneself. It is out there, in the world, it is a quality of the world given to percep-tion (just as are the paths to the possible goals, the possi-bilities themselves and the exigences of objects — books that ought to be read, shoes to be re-soled, etc.), it is the noetic correlate of the activity we have undertaken — or have only conceived.

We can now conceive what an emotion is. It is a transform-ation of the world. When the paths before us become too difficult, or when we cannot see our way, we can no longer put up with such an exacting and difficult world. All ways are barred and nevertheless we must act. So then we try to change the world; that is, to live it as though the relations between things and their potentialities were not governed by deterministic processes but by magic. But, be it well understood, this is no playful matter: we are cornered, and we fling ourselves into this new attitude with all the force at our command. Note also that our effort is not conscious of what it is, for then it would be the object of a reflection. It is above all the seizure of new relationships and new demands. To put it simply, since the seizure of one object is impossible, or sets up an unbearable tension, the consciousness seizes or tries to seize it otherwise; that is, tries to transform itself in order to transform the object. In itself, this change in the direction of the consciousness is nothing remarkable. We can find numerous examples of similar transformations of activity and of perception. For instance, to search for a shape that is dissimulated in a picture-puzzle (where is the gun?) is to deploy one's perceptivity towards the picture in a new way, it is to scan the branches, the telegraph posts, etc., in the picture *as if* one were looking at a gun, it is to carry out the ocular movements that one would make in seeing a gun. But we do not perceive these movements as such. By means of them, an intuition which transcends them, and of which they constitute the *hyle*, scrutinizes the trees and posts that are seized upon as 'possible guns' until suddenly the perception crystallizes and the gun appears. Thus, through a change of intention, as in a change of behaviour, we apprehend an object, new or old, in a different fashion. We need not first take up a position on the reflective plane. The instructions under the picture provide the immediate motivation; and we look for the gun without leaving the non-reflective plane: a potential gun has appeared, vaguely localized in the picture.

It is in this same way that we must conceive the change of

intention and of behaviour which characterizes emotion. The impossibility of finding a solution to the problem is apprehended objectively, as a quality of the world. This serves to motivate the new unreflective consciousness which now grasps the world differently, under a new aspect, and imposes a new behaviour – through which that aspect is grasped – and this again serves as *hyle* for the new intention. But emotional conduct is not on the same plane as other kinds of behaviour; it is not *effectual*. Its aim is not really to act upon the object as it is, by the interpolation of particular means. Emotional behaviour seeks by itself, and without modifying the structure of the object, to confer another quality upon it, a lesser existence or a lesser presence (or a greater existence, etc.). In a word, during emotion, it is the body which, directed by the consciousness, changes its relationship with the world so that the world should change its qualities. If emotion is playacting, the play is one that we believe in.

A simple example will serve to explain this emotive structure: I lift my hand to pluck a bunch of grapes. I cannot do so; they are beyond my reach; so I shrug my shoulders, muttering: 'they are too green', and go on my way. The gestures, words and behaviour are not to be taken at face value. This little comedy that I play under the grapes, thereby conferring this quality of being 'too green' upon them, serves as a substitute for the action I cannot complete. They presented themselves at first as 'ready for gathering'; but this attractive quality soon becomes intolerable when the potentiality cannot be actualized. The disagreeable tension becomes, in its turn, a motive for seeing another quality in those grapes: their being 'too green', which will resolve the conflict and put an end to the tension. Only, I cannot confer this quality upon the grapes chemically. So I seize upon the tartness of grapes that are too green by putting on the behaviour of disrelish. I confer the required quality upon the grapes magically. In this case the comedy is only half sincere. But let the situation be more critical; let the incantatory behaviour be maintained in all seriousness: and there you have emotion.

Take, for example, passive fear. I see a ferocious beast coming towards me: my legs give way under me, my heart beats more feebly, I turn pale, fall down and faint away. No conduct could seem worse adapted to the danger than this, which leaves me defenceless. And nevertheless it is a behaviour of *escape*; the fainting away is a refuge. But let no one suppose that it is a refuge *for me*, that I am trying to save *myself* or to *see no more* of the ferocious beast. I have not come out of the non-reflective plane: but, being unable to escape the danger by normal means and deterministic procedures, I have denied existence to it. I have tried to annihilate it. The urgency of the danger was the motive for this attempt to annihilate it, which called for magical behaviour. And, in the event, I have annihilated it so far as was in my power. Such are the limitations of my magical power over the world: I can suppress it as an object of consciousness, but only by suppressing consciousness itself.[1] Let it not be thought that the physiological behaviour in passive fear is pure disorder. It represents an abrupt realisation of the bodily conditions which ordinarily accompany the passage from the waking state to sleep.

Flight, in active fear, is mistakenly supposed to be rational behaviour. It is thought to contain calculation − admittedly brief − by the subject who wants to put the greatest possible distance between the danger and himself. But that is a

[1] Or at least by modifying it: in fainting, one passes into a dreaming consciousness − that is, into one of 'unrealization'.

misunderstanding of this behaviour, which would reduce it to prudence. We do not take flight to reach shelter: we flee because we are unable to annihilate ourselves in unconsciousness. Flight is fainting away in play; it is magical behaviour which negates the dangerous object with one's whole body, by reversing the vectorial structure of the space we live in and suddenly creating a potential direction on the *other side*. It is a way of forgetting, of negating the danger. It is in precisely the same way that an untrained boxer flings himself at his adversary with his eyes shut: he wants to suppress the existence of the other's fists; by refusing to see them he symbolically eliminates their efficacy. The real meaning of fear is now becoming apparent to us. It is a consciousness whose aim is to negate something in the external world by means of magical behaviour, and will go so far as to annihilate itself in order to annihilate the object also.

Passive sadness is characterized, as we know, by dejected behaviour; there is muscular relaxation, paleness and cold at the extremities; one turns away towards some corner to sit there motionless, making the least possible contact with the world. One prefers twilight to full daylight, silence to sound, and solitude in one's room to frequented roads and public places. 'To be alone,' as they say, 'with one's sorrow.' But that is not true at all: it is good form, of course, to appear to meditate deeply over one's grief. But cases in which a sorrow is really cherished are rather rare. There is quite another reason: one of the accustomed conditions of our activity has vanished, yet we are still required to act in and upon the world *without it*. Most of the potentialities of our world (work *to be* done, people *to see*, duties of the daily round to be accomplished) remain the same. Only the means for realizing them, the paths traced over our 'hodological space' have changed. If, for example, I have just learned that I am ruined, I no longer dispose of the same means (a private car, etc.) to accomplish them. I shall have to substitute means new to me (taking the motor-bus, etc.), which is precisely what I do not want to do. My melancholy is a method of suppressing the obligation to look for these new ways, by transforming the present structure of the world, replacing it with a totally undifferentiated structure. What it comes to, in short, is that I make the world into an affectively neutral reality, a system which is, affectively, in complete equilibrium. Objects highly charged with affect are de-charged, brought down to affective zero, and therefore apprehended as perfectly equivalent and interchangeable. In other words, lacking both the ability and the will to carry out the projects I formerly entertained, I behave in such a manner that the universe requires nothing more from me. This one can do only by acting upon oneself, by 'lowering the flame of life to a pin-point' – and the noetic correlate of this attitude is what we call *Bleakness*: the universe is bleak; that is, of undifferentiated structure. At the same time, therefore, we naturally draw back into ourselves, we 'efface ourselves', and the noetic counterpart of that is the *Refuge*. The entire universe is bleak, and it is precisely in order to protect ourselves from its frightful, illimitable monotony that we make some place or other into a 'shelter'. That is the one differentiating factor in the absolute monotony of the world: a bleak wall, a little darkness to screen us from that bleak immensity.

Active sadness can take many forms; but the one cited by Janet (of the psychasthenic who throws a fit of nerves because she does not want to make her confession) may be characterized as a refusal. It exemplifies above all a negative behaviour intended to deny the urgency of certain problems and to replace them by others. The patient wants to move Janet's feelings. This means that she wants to change his attitude of impassible expectancy into one of affectionate concern. She wants this and she makes use of her body to bring it about. At the same time, by putting herself into such a state that the confession would be impossible, she is renouncing that act as beyond her power. Now, and for as long as she is in tears and shaken with her sobbing, all possibility of speaking is taken from her. Here, then, the potentiality is not eliminated, the confession remains 'to be made'. But it has retreated beyond the reach of the patient, who can no longer will to make it, but only *hope* to do so one day. The patient has thus freed herself from the painful feeling that the act was *in her power*, that she was free to do it or not. The emotional crisis here is an abandonment of responsibility, by means of a magical exaggeration of the difficulty of the world. The world retains its differentiated structure, but it appears unjust and hostile, because it is demanding *too much* of us; that is, more than it is humanly possible to do. In this case, then, the emotion of sadness is a magical play-acting of impotence: the patient is like one of those domestic servants who, having admitted burglars to their master's house, get them to bind them hand and foot, as a clear demonstration that they could not have prevented the theft. Here, however, the patient ties herself up in a number of tenuous bonds. It might be said, perhaps, that the painful sense of liberty of which the patient wants to rid herself is necessarily of a reflective nature. But this we do not believe; and one has only to watch oneself to see what really happens. It is the object which presents itself as demanding to be *freely* created; the confession which presents itself as the deed which both *ought to* and *can* be done.

There are, of course, other functions and other forms of

---

active sadness. We will say no more about anger, which we have discussed at length already, and which, of all the emotions, is perhaps the most evidently functional. But what is to be said about joy? Does it fit into our description? At first sight it would seem not, since the joyful subject has no need to defend himself against a belittling or dangerous change. But we must first distinguish between the joyful feeling which betokens an equilibrium, or a state of adaptation, and emotional joy. For the latter, on closer consideration, is characterised by a certain impatience. We mean by this that the joyful subject is behaving very much like a man in a state of impatience. He cannot keep still, makes innumerable plans, begins to do things which he immediately abandons etc. For in fact this joy has been called up by an apparition of the object of his desires. He has been told that he has won a considerable sum of money, or that he will shortly meet someone he loves and has not seen for a long time. But although the object is 'imminent' it is not yet there, it is not yet *his*. He is separated from it by a certain length of time. And even when it is present, even when the friend so long desired appears upon the station platform, he is still an object that delivers itself to one only little by little; the delight that we feel in seeing him again soon becomes blunted; we shall never get so far as to hold him there, in front of us, as our own absolute possession and to grasp him all at once as a whole (nor shall we ever realise all at once our new-won riches, as an instantaneous totality. It will yield itself to us only through numberless details and, as it were, by *abschattungen*). Joy is magical behaviour which tries, by incantation, to realize the possession of the desired object as an instantaneous totality. This behaviour is accompanied by certainty that possession will be realized sooner or later, but it seeks to anticipate that possession. The various activities expressive of joy, as well as the muscular hypertonicity and the slight vascular dilatation, are animated and transcended by an intention which envisages the world through them. This seems easy, the object of our desires appears to be near and easy to posses. Every gesture expresses emphatic approbation. To dance, or to sing for joy – these represent the behaviour of symbolic approximation, of incantation. By their means the object – which in reality one may not be able to posses except by prudent and, after all, difficult behaviour – is possessed at once, symbolically. It is thus, for example, that a man to whom a woman has just said that she loves him may begin to dance and sing. In so doing he turns his mind away from the prudent and difficult behaviour he will have to maintain if he is to deserve this love and increase it, to gain possession of it through countless details (smiles, little attentions etc.). He turns away even from the woman herself as the living reality representative of all those delicate procedures. Those he will attend to later; he is now giving himself a rest. For the moment, he is possessing the object by magic; the dance mimes his possession of it.

However, we cannot be quite content with these few observations. They have enabled us to appreciate the functional part played by emotion, but still we do not know very much about its nature.

We must note first of all that the few examples we have cited are far from having exhausted all the varieties of emotion. Many other fears are possible, many other kinds of sadness. We are only affirming that they are all reducible to the constitution of a magic world, by making use of our bodies as instruments of incantation. In every case the problem is different, and the behaviour is different. To grasp the signification and aim, one would have to know and analyse each particular situation. Broadly speaking, there are not four principal types of emotion: there are many more, and it would be a useful and productive work to classify them. For example, if the fear of a timid person changes suddenly into anger (change of conduct motivated by a change in the situation), this anger is not of the ordinary type: it is *fear surpassed*. This does not mean at all that it is in some way reducible to fear, but simply that it retains the antecedent fear included in its own structure. But it is only when one is persuaded of the functional character of emotion that one can arrive at an understanding of the infinite variety of states of emotional consciousness. On the other hand, we ought never to lose sight of one capital fact: that behaviour pure and simple is *not* emotion, any more than is the pure and simple awareness of that behaviour. If it were so, indeed, the finalist character of emotion would be far more clearly apparent and, on the other hand, consciousness could easily free itself from emotion. Moreover, there are spurious emotions which are nothing more than behaviour. If someone gives me a present in which I am only half interested, I may make an outward show of intense delight; I may clap my hands, jump or dance. This however is only play-acting. I let myself be a little carried away by it, and it would be inaccurate to say that I am *not* joyful; nevertheless, my delight is not genuine, I shall throw it off as soon as my visitor has gone. This is precisely what we call *false* joy, bearing in mind that falsity is not a logical characteristic of certain propositions but an existential quality. In the same sense I can have false fears, false sorrows. Such false states of mind are however quite distinct from those of the actor: an actor imitates joy, sorrow etc., without *being* joyful or sorrowful, for his behaviour is addressed to a fictional world. He imitates behaviour but is not himself behaving. In the various cases of false emotion that I have just mentioned, the behaviour is not sustained by anything, it exists alone and is voluntary: but the situation is real and is thought to require such behaviour. Moreover, through such behaviour we magic-ally 'will' certain qualities upon real objects: but those qual-ities are false.

It must not be supposed that they are therefore imaginary, nor that they are bound to vanish away later. Their falsity is that of an essential weakness pretending to be violence. My pleasure in the object I have just been given exists much more as a duty than as a reality; it has a sort of parasitic reality as a tribute, of that I am very well aware; I know that I am endowing the object with it by a kind of fascination, but when I desist from my incantations this will immediately disappear.

Real emotion is quite another matter: it is accompanied by belief. The qualities 'willed' upon the objects are taken to be real. What exactly is to be understood by that? This – or almost this – that the emotion is undergone. One cannot get out of it as one pleases; it fades away of itself, but one cannot put a stop to it. Furthermore, the behaviour, viewed simply in itself, imprints upon the object no more than a schematic suggestion of the quality one is attributing to it. Merely to run away from it would not be enough to constitute an object as horrifying. Or rather, this might confer the formal quality 'horrifying' upon it, but not the substance of that quality. If we are really to be seized by horror we have not only to mime it, we must be spell-bound and filled to overflowing by our own emotion, the shape and form of our behaviour must be filled with something opaque and weighty that gives it substance. Here we can understand the part played by the purely physiological phenomena; they represent the *genuineness* of the emotion, they are the phenomena of belief. True, they must not be separated from the behaviour: in the first place, they present a certain analogy with it. The hypotonicity in fear or in sadness, the vascular constrictions and respiratory troubles are symbolical enough, together with a behaviour which is trying to negate the world or to discharge it of its potential by negating itself. It is hence impossible to mark exactly the frontier between pure troubles and behaviour. And secondly, they combine with the behaviour in one whole synthetic form and are not to be studied for their own sake. To have considered them in isolation was precisely the error of the peripheric theory. And nevertheless, they are not reducible to behaviour: one can stop oneself from running, but not from trembling. I can, by a violent effort, rise from my chair, dismiss from my mind the disaster that has overcome me and set myself to work; but my hands remain ice-cold. Emotion, then, cannot be regarded simply as play-acting; it is not mere behaviour, but the behaviour of a body which is in a specific state: the state itself would not give rise to the behaviour, the behaviour without the state is play-acting; but the emotion appears in a disordered body carrying on a certain kind of behaviour. The bodily disturbance may continue longer than the behaviour, but the behaviour constitutes the form and the signification of the disorder. On the other hand, the behaviour without this disorder would be mere signification, an emotional schema. The form we have to do with is indeed synthetic: *to believe* in magical behaviour one must be physically upset.

Clearly to understand the emotional process as it proceeds from consciousness, we must remember the dual nature of the body, which on the one hand is an object in the world and on the other is immediately *lived* by the consciousness. Only then can we grasp what is essential – that emotion is a phenomenon of belief. Consciousness does not limit itself to the projection of affective meanings upon the world around it; it *lives* the new world it has thereby constituted – lives it directly, commits itself to it, and suffers from the qualities that the concomitant behaviour has outlined. This means that, all ways out being barred, the consciousness leaps into the magical world of emotion, plunges wholly into it by debasing itself. It becomes a different consciousness confronting a different world – a world which it constitutes with its own most intimate quality, with that presence to itself, utterly non-distant, of its point of view upon the world. A consciousness becoming emotional is rather like a consciousness dropping asleep. The one, like the other, slips into another world and transforms the body as a synthetic whole so as to be able to live and to perceive this other world through it. In other words, the consciousness changes its body, or, to put it another way, the body – considered as the point of view upon the universe immediately inherent in consciousness – is raised to the level of the behaviour. That is why the physiological manifestations are, at bottom, disorders of the most ordinary description; they resemble those of fever, of angina pectoris, of artificial over-excitation etc. They merely represent a complete and commonplace upset of the body, such as it is (the behaviour alone will decide whether this disarray is to be a 'diminishment' of life or an 'amplification' of it). In itself it is nothing, it represents no more than an obscuration of the conscious point of view upon the world, in so far as the consciousness realizes and *spontaneously* lives this obscuration. It is advisable, naturally to understand this obscuration as a synthetic phenomenon, as indivisible.

But since, on the other hand, the body is a thing among things, a scientific analysis may be able to distinguish, in the biological body, in the body as a thing, the local disorder of this or that organ.

Thus the origin of emotion is a spontaneous debasement lived by consciousness in face of the world. What it is unable to endure in one way it tries to seize in another way, by going to sleep, by reducing itself to the states of consciousness in sleep, dream or hysteria. And the bodily disturbance is nothing else than the belief lived by the consciousness, as it is seen from outside. Only, it must be noted:

First, that the consciousness has no thetic consciousness of self as abasing itself to escape the pressures of the world; it has only a positional consciousness of the degradation of the world, which has passed over to the magical plane. Still, a non-thetic consciousness of itself remains. It is to the degree that it does so, and to that degree only, that we can say of an emotion that it is not sincere. It is not at all surprising, therefore, that the final aim of an emotion is not posited by an act of consciousness in the midst of the emotion itself. Its finality is not for all that unconscious, but it is 'used up' in the constituting of the object.

Secondly, that the consciousness is caught in its own snare. Precisely because it is living in the new aspect of the world by believing in it, the consciousness is captured by its own belief, exactly as it is in dreams and hysteria. The consciousness of the emotion is captive, but by this it must not be understood to be fettered by anything whatever outside itself. It is captive to itself in this sense – that it does not dominate the belief that it is doing its utmost to live, and this precisely because it is living that belief and is absorbed in living it. It must not be imagined that consciousness is spontaneous in the sense that it is always free to deny a thing and to affirm it at one and the same moment. Such a spontaneity would be self-contradictory. It is of the essence of consciousness to transcend itself, and it is therefore impossible for it to withdraw within itself and to doubt whether it is outside in the object. It knows itself only in the world. And doubt, of its very nature, can be nothing but the constitution of an existential quality of the object; the doubtful, or the reflective activity of reduction – that is, the property of a new consciousness directed towards the positional consciousness. Thus, when consciousness is living the magical world into which it has precipitated itself, it tends to perpetuate that world, by which it is captivated: the emotion tends to perpetuate itself. It is in this sense that we may say it is undergone; the consciousness is moved by its emotion and heightens it. The faster one flees the more one is afraid. The magical world appears, takes form, and then closes in on the consciousness and clutches it: it cannot even wish to escape, it may seek to flee from the magical object, but to flee from it is to give it more magical reality than ever. And this very condition of captivity is not in itself realized by the consciousness, which attributes it to the objects – it is they that are captivating, imprisoning it, they have taken possession of the consciousness. Liberation can come only from a purifying reflection or from the total disappearance of the emotional situation.

Nevertheless and for all that, emotion would not be so all-absorbing if it apprehended in the object no more than the exact counterpart of what it is noetically (for instance, at this present time, in this light, in such or such circumstances, this man is terrifying). But it is constitutive of emotion that it attributes to the object something that infinitely transcends it. Indeed, there is a world of emotion. All emotions have this in common, that they evoke the appearance of a world, cruel, terrible, bleak, joyful, etc., but in which the relations of things to consciousness are always and exclusively magical. We have to speak of a world of emotion as one speaks of a world of dreams or of worlds of madness. A world – that means individual syntheses in mutual relations and possessing *qualities*. But no quality is conferred upon an object without passing over to the infinite. This grey, for instance, represents the units of an infinity of real and possible *abschattungen*, some of which will be grey-green, some grey seen in a certain light, black, etc. Similarly, the qualities that emotion confers upon the object and upon the world, it confers upon them *ad aeternum*. True, when I suddenly conceive an object to be horrible I do not explicitly affirm that it will remain horrible for eternity. But the mere affirmation of horribleness as a substantial quality of the object is already, in itself, a passage to the infinite. The horrible is now in the thing, at the heart of it, is its emotive texture, is constitutive of it. Thus, during emotion an overwhelming and definitive quality of the thing makes its appearance. And that is what transcends and maintains our emotion. Horribleness is not only the present state of the thing, it is a menace for the future, it extends over and darkens the whole future, it is a revelation about the meaning of the world. The 'horrible' means indeed that horribleness is a substantial quality, that there is horribleness in the world. Thus, in every emotion, a multitude of affective protensions extends into the future and presents it in an emotional light. We are living, emotively, a quality that penetrates into us, that we are suffering, and that surrounds us in every direction. Immediately, the emotion is lifted out of itself and transcends itself; it is no ordinary episode of our daily life, but an intuition of the absolute.

It is this that explains the subtle emotions. In these, by means of a hardly noticeable behaviour, through a slight oscillation of our physical condition, we apprehend an objective quality of the object. Subtle emotion is not at all afraid of the slightly unpleasant, of a diminished excellence or of what is superficially disastrous: for it only *glimpses* the unpleasant, the excellent or the disastrous through a veil. It is a dim intuition, and presents itself as such. But the object is there, waiting; and tomorrow perhaps the veil will be withdrawn and we shall see it in full daylight. Therefore one may be very little moved – if by moved we understand all those disturbances of the body or the behaviour – and still apprehend our whole life as disastrous. The disaster is total, we know it, it is profound; but for the present we have only a glimpse of it. In this case and in many others like it, the emotion seems to be much stronger than it really is, since, in spite of all, we sense a profound disaster through it. These subtle emotions are, naturally, tangentially different from the merely weak emotions which invest the object with no more than a faintly affective character. It is the intention that differentiates subtle from weak emotion, for the behaviour and the somatic condition may be identical in both cases. But the intention is, in its turn, motivated by the situation.

This theory of emotion does not explain the immediate reactions of horror and wonder that sometimes possess us when certain objects suddenly appear to us. For example, a grimacing face suddenly appears pressed against the outside of the window; I am frozen with terror. Here, of course, there is no appropriate behaviour and it would seem that the emotion has no finality. Moreover, in a general way, our apprehension of the horrible in situations or faces is more or less immediate and is not usually manifested by flight, or by fainting: one is not even tempted to flee. Nevertheless, upon closer consideration, these very peculiar phenomena are susceptible of an explanation compatible with the ideas we have been discussing. We have seen how, during an emotion, the consciousness abases itself and abruptly transmutes the determinist world in which we live, into a magical world. But, conversely, sometimes it is this world that reveals itself to consciousness as magical just where we expect it to be deterministic. It must not, indeed, be supposed that magic is an ephemeral quality that we impose upon the world according to our humour. There is an existential structure of the world which is magical. We will not now enlarge upon this subject, which we are reserving for treatment elsewhere. However, we are able here and now to point out that the category of 'magic' governs the interpsychic relations between men in society and, more precisely, our perception of others. The magical, as Alain says, is 'the mind crawling among things'; that is, an irrational synthesis of spontaneity and passivity. It is an inert activity, a consciousness rendered passive. But it is precisely in that form that others appear to us, and this, not because of our position in relation to them, nor in consequence of our passions, but by essential necessity. Indeed, consciousness can only be a transcendent object by undergoing the modification of passivity. Thus the meaning of a face is, first of all, that of the consciousness (not a sign of the consciousness) but of a consciousness that is altered, degraded − which precisely is passivity. We will return to these remarks later, when we hope to show that they impose themselves upon the mind. It follows that man is always a sorcerer to man and the social world is primarily magical. Not that it is impossible to take a deterministic view of the interpsychological world or to build rational superstructures upon it. But then it is those structures that are ephemeral and unstable, it is they that crumble away as soon as the magical aspect of faces, gestures and human situations becomes too vivid. And what happens then, when the superstructures laboriously built up by the reason disintegrate, and man finds himself suddenly plunged back again into the original magic? That is easily predicted; the consciousness seizes upon the magic as magic, and lives it vividly as such. The categories 'suspicious' and 'disquieting', etc. designate the magical, in so far as it is being lived by consciousness or tempting consciousness to live it.

The sudden passage from a rational apprehension of the world to an apprehension of the same world as magical, when this is motivated by the object itself and accompanied by a disagreeable element — that is horror: if it is accompanied by an agreeable element, it will be admiration (we mention these two examples, but there are naturally many other cases). Thus there are two forms of emotion, according to whether it is we who constitute the magic of the world to replace a determin-istic activity which cannot be realized, or whether the world itself is unrealizable and reveals itself suddenly as a magical environment. In the state of horror, we are suddenly made aware that the deterministic barriers have given way. That face which appears at the window, for instance — we do not at first take it as that of a man, who might push the door open and take thirty paces to where we are standing. On the contrary, it is presented, motionless though it is, as acting at a distance. The face outside the window is in immediate relationship with our body; we are living and undergoing its signification; it is with our own flesh that we constitute it, but at the same time it imposes itself, annihilates the distance and enters into us. Consciousness plunged into this magic world drags the body with it in as much as the body is belief and the consciousness believes in it. The behaviour which gives its meaning to the emotion is no longer *our* behaviour; it is the expression of the face and the movements of the body of the other being, which make up a synthetic whole together with the upheaval in our own organism. Here again, then, we find the same elements and the same structure as we were describing a little while ago, except that in the former case the magic and the meaning of the emotion came from the world and not from ourselves. Naturally, magic, as a real quality of the world, is not strictly limited to the human. It extends to things also, inasmuch as they may present themselves as human (the disturbing impression of a landscape, of certain objects, or of a room which retains the traces of some mysterious visitor) or bear the imprint of the psychic. And, also naturally, the two main types of emotion are not absolutely and strictly distinct; there are often mixtures of the two types and the majority of our emotions are less than pure. Thus it is that the consciousness which is realizing, with spontaneous finality, a magical aspect of the world may create the opportunity to manifest itself as a real magical quality. And reciprocally, if the world presents itself as magical in one way or another, it may be the consciousness that specifies and achieves the constitution of this magic and is diffusing it everywhere or, on the contrary, is concentrating it forcibly upon a single object.

In any case, it must be noted that emotion is not the accidental modification of a subject who is surrounded by an unchanged world. It is easy to see that no emotional apprehension of an object as frightening, irritating, saddening, etc. can arise except against the background of a complete alteration of the world. For an object to appear *formidable*, indeed, it must be realized as an immediate and magical presence confronting the consciousness. For example, this face that I see ten yards away behind the window must be lived as an immediate, present threat to myself. But this is possible only in an act of consciousness which destroys all the structures of the world that might dispel the magic and reduce the event to reasonable proportions. It would require, for instance, that the window as 'object that must first be broken' and the ten yards as 'distance that must first be covered' should be annihilated. This does not mean in the least that the consciousness in its terror brings the face nearer, in the sense of reducing the distance between it and my body. To reduce a distance is still to be thinking in terms of distance. Similarly, although the terrified subject might think, about the window, 'it could easily be broken', or 'it could be opened from outside', these are only rational explanations that he might offer for his fear. In reality, the window and the distance are seized simultaneously in the act of consciousness which catches sight of the face at the window: but in this very act of catching sight of it, window and distance are emptied of their necessary character as tools. They are grasped in another way. The distance is no longer grasped as distance – for it is not thought of as 'that which would first have to be traversed', it is grasped as the background united with the horrible. The window is no longer grasped as 'that which would first have to be opened', it is grasped simply as the frame of the frightful visage. And in a general way, areas form themselves around me out of which the horrible makes itself felt. For the horrible is not possible in the deterministic world of tools. The horrible can appear only in a world which is such that all the things existing in it are magical by nature, and the only defences against them are magical. This is what we experience often enough in the universe of dreams, where doors, locks and walls are no protection against the threats of robbers or wild animals for they are all grasped in one and the same act of horror. And since the act which is to disarm them is the same as that which is creating them, we see the assassins passing through doors and walls; we press the trigger of our revolver in vain, no shot goes off. In a word, to experience any object as horrible, is to see it against the background of a world which reveals itself as *already* horrible.

Thus consciousness can 'be-in-the-world' in two different ways. The world may appear before it as an organized complex of utilizable things, such that, if one wants to produce a predetermined effect, one must act upon the determinate elements of that complex. As one does so, each 'tool' refers one to other tools and to the totality of tools; there is no absolute action, no radical change that one can introduce immediately into this world. We have to modify one particular tool, and this by means of another which refers in its turn to yet another, and so on to infinity. But the world may also confront us at one nonutilizable whole; that is, as only modifiable without intermediation and by great masses. In that case, the categories of the world act immediately upon the consciousness, they are present to it *at no distance* (for example, the face that frightens us through the window acts upon us *without* any means; there is no need for the window to open, for a man to leap into the room or to walk across the floor). And, conversely, the consciousness tries to combat these dangers or to modify these objects at no distance and without means, by some absolute, massive modification of the world. This aspect of the world is an entirely coherent one; this is the *magical* world. Emotion may be called a sudden fall of consciousness into magic; or, if you will, emotion arises when the world of the utilizable vanishes abruptly and the world of magic appears in its place. We must not, therefore, see in emotion a passing disorder of the organism and the mind which enters and upsets them *from outside*. On the contrary, it is the return of consciousness to the magical attitude, one of the great attitudes which are essential to it, with the appearance of the correlative world – the magical world. Emotion is not an accident, it is a mode of our conscious existence, one of the ways in which consciousness understands (in Heidegger's sense of *Verstehen*) its Being-in-the-World.

A reflective consciousness can always direct its attention upon emotion. In that case, emotion is seen as a structure of consciousness. It is not a pure, ineffable quality like brick-red or the pure feeling of pain – as it would have to be according to James's theory. It has a meaning, it *signifies something for my psychic life*. The purifying reflection of phenomenological reduction enables us to perceive emotion at work constituting the magical form of the world. 'I find him hateful *because* I am angry.' But that reflection is rare, and depends upon special motivations. In the ordinary way, the reflection that we direct towards the emotive consciousness is accessory after the fact. It may indeed recognize the consciousness *qua* consciousness, but only as it is motivated by the object: 'I am angry because *he* is hateful.' It is from that kind of reflection that passion is constituted.

CONCLUSION

The theory of the emotions outlined in the preceding pages
was intended to serve as an experiment for the constitution of
a phenomenological psychology. Naturally, its character as an
example has prevented our entering upon the developments
to which it should lead.[1] On the other hand, since it was
necessary to make a clean sweep of the ordinary psychological theories of emotion, we have had to ascend gradually
from the psychological considerations of James to the idea of
signification. A phenomenological psychology which was
sure of itself, and had already cleared the ground, would
begin by first of all establishing, in an eidetic reflection, the
essence of the psychological fact it was investigating. That is

---

[1] From this point of view, we hope that our suggestions may lead, in particular, to the initiation of complete monographic studies of joy, sadness,
etc. Here we have furnished only the schematic directions of such
monographs.

what we have tried to do for the *mental image* in a work that will shortly appear. But in spite of these reservations of detail, we hope we have succeeded in showing that a psychological fact like emotion, commonly supposed to be a lawless disorder, possesses a signification of its own, and cannot be understood in itself, without the comprehension of this signification. We now wish to indicate the limitations of such a psychological investigation.

We said, in our Introduction, that the significance of a fact of consciousness came to this: that it always pointed to the whole human-reality which was *making* itself emotional, attentive, perceptive, willing, etc. The study of the emotions has indeed verified this principle: an emotion refers to what it signifies. And what it signifies is indeed, in effect, the totality of the relations of the human-reality to the world. The onset of emotion is a complete modification of the 'being-in-the-world' according to the very particular laws of magic. But one can immediately see the limitations of such a description: the psychological theory of emotion postulates an antecedent description of affectivity so far as the latter constitutes the being of the human-reality – that is, in so far as it is constitutive of our human-reality to be affective human-reality. If that postulate were granted, then instead of beginning with a study of emotion or of the inclinations that pointed to a human-reality not yet elucidated as the ultimate term of all research – an ideal term, moreover, and very probably unattainable for those who start from the empirical – our description of the affects would *proceed* from the human-reality described and fixed by an *a priori* intuition. The various disciplines of phenomenological psychology are *regressive* although though the ultimate term of their regression is, for them, purely ideal: those of pure phenomenology, on the contrary, are progressive. It may, no doubt, be asked why, under these conditions, one should choose to employ the two disciplines simultaneously; pure phenomenology might seem to suffice. But, if phenomenology can prove that emotion is realization of the essence of the human-reality in so far as the latter is *affectivity*, it will be impossible for it to show that the human-reality must necessarily manifest itself in *such* emotions as it does. That there are such and such emotions and not others – this is, beyond all doubt, evidence of the *factitious* character of human existence. It is this factitiousness that necessitates a regular recourse to the empirical; and which, in all probability, will forever prevent the psychological regression and the phenomenological progression from complete convergence.

Printed in the United States
by Baker & Taylor Publisher Services